The War Makes Everyone Lonely

PHOENIX POETS

GRAHAM BARNHART

The War Makes Everyone Lonely

THE UNIVERSITY OF CHICAGO PRESS
Chicago & London

The University of Chicago Press, Chicago 60637
The University of Chicago Press, Ltd., London

Published 2019
Printed in the United States of America

28 27 26 25 24 23 22 21 20 2 3 4 5

ISBN-13: 978-0-226-66046-2 (paper)
ISBN-13: 978-0-226-66063-9 (e-book)
DOI: https://doi.org/10.7208/chicago/9780226660639.001.0001

Library of Congress Cataloging-in-Publication Data

Names: Barnhart, Graham, author.
Title: The war makes everyone lonely / Graham Barnhart.
Other titles: Phoenix poets.
Description: Chicago ; London : The University of Chicago Press, 2019. | Series: Phoenix poets
Identifiers: LCCN 2019008628 | ISBN 9780226660462 (pbk. : alk. paper) | ISBN 9780226660639 (e-book)
Subjects: LCSH: Afghan War, 2001—Poetry. | Iraq War, 2003–2011—Poetry. | War poetry, American. | LCGFT: Poetry.
Classification: LCC PS3602.A83445 A6 2019 | DDC 811/.6—dc23
LC record available at https://lccn.loc.gov/2019008628

♾ This paper meets the requirements of ANSI/NISO Z39.48-1992 (Permanence of Paper).

for T

You are not a witness to the ruin.
You are the ruin to be witnessed.

Robert Persons, *General Orders No. 9*

CONTENTS

ACKNOWLEDGMENTS

Grateful acknowledgment is made to the following publications in which versions of these poems first appeared:

32 Poems: "Informant" (formerly titled "Informant [Name Redacted]") and "Survival and Evasion"
Adroit Journal: "Goat in the Cleared Village"
Beloit Poetry Journal: "Call to Prayer," "Pissing in Irbil," "The Road to Pol-e-Khomri," and "What Being in the Army Did"
The Boiler: "Unpracticed"
Diagram: "Aubade between Deployments"
Diode: "Shura"
Gettysburg Review: "Belated Letter to My Grandmother" and "Notice and Focus Exercise"
Gulf Coast: "How to Stop the Bleeding"
Horsethief Books: "Tinder Pic"
Iowa Review: "The War Makes Everyone Lonely," "Sewing," "My Pittsburgh," "Days of 2009," "Certificates of Training," "Indiana-stan," "Cultivating Mass," and "Everything in Sunlight I Can't Stop Seeing"
Pleiades: "Days of Spring, 2016"
Poetry Northwest: "Pashtu Refresher"
Prelude: "Blocking an Imagined War Movie"
Sewanee Review: "1900" (formerly titled "Sentry Meditation: 2300") and "0300" (formerly titled "Sentry Meditation: 0100")
Sycamore Review: "Post 9/11 Gas Training" (presented here in two parts)

Tinderbox Poetry Journal: "The Coffee Aisle" and "Deserving" (presented here in two parts)
Waxwing Literary Journal: "Breach" and "A Fable"

I am endlessly thankful

to my family, my parents Kathy and Joe, my siblings Brennan, Devon, Logan, Drew, and Darin, and especially my grandparents Pap and Betty;

to my teachers Jim Bulman, Eavan Boland, Henri Cole, the faculty at the Ohio State University Creative Writing Department and at the Stegner Fellowship, Carolyn Forché, Adam Johnson, and Patrick Phillips, for their immense generosity;

to friend and mentor Christopher Bakken, without whom it is safe to say I would not be a poet;

to Alan Shapiro, for his advocacy and support in helping to realize this book;

to Allegheny College, the creative writing programs at Ohio State University and Stanford University, Bread Loaf Writers' Conference, and Writing Workshops in Greece, for all of their generous financial and educational support;

to everyone at Pension Archodissa, for years of divine hospitality, friendship, and *tsipouro*;

and to the cohorts, friends, and confederates at Ohio State and Stanford, for their community, advice, and patience.

I would like to make special acknowledgment to *Beloit Poetry Journal*, for publishing my first poems and awarding them the Chad Walsh Poetry Prize. Gratitude also to *Iowa Review*, for their support of the Jeff Sharlet Memorial Award for Veterans, and to Phil Klay, for choosing my poems.

Lastly, to 32 and 21, thank you for putting up with my shit, for keeping me alive on this earth, and for showing me how to be a soldier—our version of that, at least.

The War Makes Everyone Lonely

BELATED LETTER TO MY GRANDMOTHER

You wrote to ask if it was hot,
if the work was hard, if I was staying safe,
and I could have answered.
When the flag above the Perkins was torn,
harrowed by a storm in January,
you told the men wrestling a new one
onto the pole that something smaller
would rip less often. You were right. I'm sorry
I never wrote while I was away—I thought only tragedy
makes us interesting—but I would have told you
about the black garbage scraps in the barbwire,
brittle, thrumming, always on the verge of flight;
that I saw few birds there but many hornets;
and when the air moved, I could see it.
And no, I don't think I was afraid of dying.
Seven months isn't so long a time. Unlike life,
war can be survived. Like walking in the dark.
Not frightened, just tentative, trying not to step
in a bear trap. Home now, it's different: still
dark but fewer traps. Decisions take more
time and are easier to forget. You always said
dull knives are more dangerous—
I grow duller every day. Mornings are steam
in the coffee press. Afternoons come hushing
through pines to pool like rain in the porch chairs.
I like them empty, leaf shadow mottling the grass.

I like the highway when I convince myself it could
be waves against a far, lanterned shore.
You would too, I think . . . and my neighbor's son
practicing oboe. Most of the time
he sounds like a robot learning to speak,
but now and then an almost "Ode to Joy"
or "Lean on Me" outlines itself, and I forget
I am going to die. That we all are, and probably
nothing happens after, so we won't mind or notice,
and what I'm really afraid of isn't dying, but now
it's "Hey Jude." It's very probably "Hey Jude" most
of the time, and, anyway, he's better than me, more diligent.
When I was pretending to learn piano, I played melodies
I already knew and had, you said, no patience
for mystery. Why keep tracing the constellations?
So I wanted to tell you about him, this kid next door
who plays what could be anything, and to say yes,
yes, the guns were loud—loud like gods applauding.

WHAT BEING IN THE ARMY DID

Things you'd expect.
Taught me a trigger's weight—

its pull—depends on the gun
and doesn't matter much

if you practice
proper follow-through.

Follow-through here means holding
the squeeze through the kick

like you won't have to do it again,
like you'll never have to do it again.

The army taught me torsos
and tailgates

are useful for gauging distance.
That swaying grass

or flags or neckties
can estimate wind speed,

and traveling from an artifact
to a fundamental constant

requires loss.
It takes me sixty steps

to walk one hundred meters.
Assuming my body weight

and leg lengths remain
roughly constant,

and I'm using a compass,
which means I'm moving

in very straight lines, then sixty
ten times is a kilometer,

and sixty one hundred times is ten.

In France, they have a lump
of platinum and iridium made in 1879.

They named it Le Grand K,
and that's how much a kilogram is.

They keep it under glass.
Won't even touch it wearing gloves

because of however much
a fingerprint weighs.

They used to have a metal rod
about three feet long,

now a meter is how fast light travels
in 1/299,792,458ths of a second.

Five liters is still the same
as a little over a gallon,

but any amount of blood looks
like more blood than it is.

When I say things like that
my girlfriend asks

if I'm proud of being dangerous.
I can safely say

I used to be and now at least
I know the dull machine chunk

of a rifle's sear reset between rounds,
a sound my father asked about once.

He asked if I knew any words
that sound like a prison door locking.

Abduction? Deconstruction?
I imagined many syllables

tumbling.
He shook his head.

So I said maybe there is no word.
Maybe if there are bars

describe the feeling
of the air between them.

If there are keys, the distance
between the sound of them

touching and the sound
of them touching the door.

The weight of your days
approaching that closure—

No, he said,
there is definitely a word.

WHAT'S IT LIKE?

We have made *unspeakable* mean indescribable:
it really means nasty.

I don't mean nasty. I mean today
a fresh ejected .50-cal. casing,
hot brass thick round as a lipstick shuttle,
coerced new blisters from my neck, and earlier
leaves stirred in wind I couldn't feel
as I watched a camel through a scope
bend down dying. I mean the chirps,
whistles, and wind drawn trilling
from rooftop vents of the abandoned
Red Cross warehouse—in its empty compound
next to ours—were indistinguishable
from song thrush nesting in the concertina.

CALL TO PRAYER

Closer than a church bell's dismantling. A stillness
raveled rather than torn. I expected violence

brought forth upon good rust and megaphones,
command wire, unfastened earth, and buried yellow jugs.

I expected old men around gas-fed heaters to turn
their faces away from me, and children to throw stones,

but not the young boy at the hand-pump water well
kneeling beside his bucket to kiss the dirt.

Even the sun arrests its tilting, shade pools at the minaret's base
like thawed ice running out from stones.

I did not expect the song to be lamb smoke wandering
paper thin between the furrows of sunset-hammered

rice and poppy—a drifting current of lemon through red wine,
a ribbon sometimes

touching the lips—obliging the lips to touch the hands,
the forehead the ground.

AUBADE BETWEEN DEPLOYMENTS

What comprehension is required? I dream
of horses in a field of soldiers sleeping.
Mist and the morning ravines release
like fists disappearing. Awake, I can't decide
which of the hands was letting go, or if I am
awake, hammock strung on the handles
of two MAT-Vs, when—gentle
                                        as any wild animal
threatens not to be—a horse shoulders against me.
A dream horse would do this. A real horse
might, but that mist, lifting now
from the flattened grass, lifting from its
chestnut coat, wouldn't need to mean
anything. If it breathes,
                              it breathes softly.

1900

Early in the season of peace, winter
fends off the war. High passes spill over
with clattering wind like brass shells from children's
pockets. Boat lamps on dark water, village
fires and porch lights gather silently
at dusk. What makes one foreign place seem like
another? The Greek island. Its rippling sheets
of corrugated sunlight. The moon-white
marble quarry. The ashes still washing
into beach sand a year after the fire.
Lightning encouraged the pines to light.
Cones burst their seeds in clouds of burning flak.
Families stood on rooftops with garden
hoses fanning their steaming goats. Beards burned.
On the mountain Kleftoyannis, named
for John the Thief, black olive trunks drift smokelike
from scoured terraces. Their hollows curling
bent silhouettes of mouths shocked into song.
It isn't all gone to soot, cicadas
still go on grinding somehow, escaping
their onion-skin husks. Grapevines drip greenly
from seaside trellises of the gutted
summer pensions. They tangle in clotheslines
and shiver in rain like unfurled peacocks.
Those birds still peal their horrific alarms
from bare branches, and the moon, relentless,

still quarters and halves itself above them.
That white improbable horse still nibbles
in its low, surviving grove, and the boat,
the blue painted rowboat, has been replaced
on the rocks. Seagulls drift alternating
pale and shadowed varieties of ash
toward fishermen emptying their nets.
Is it Thales of Miletus who said
the world is made of water? He's famous
for that and for falling into a well
while giving a lecture about the stars.
Imagine a long stone barrel, a ring
of sky, a few caught stars and any belief
tangible enough to fall into
when headlights scroll the only open road
between hills named to expedite mortars:
X-ray, Juliet, Hotel, Romeo.
Recite their names. Your catalog of fire.

PISSING IN IRBIL

Behind me a Kurdish woman
holding cherries in a plastic bag
rustles gravel the way

you might clear your throat
if you caught a foreign soldier
pissing in side-alley rubble

that had been the walls and ceiling
and staircase of your home. Even rocks
drag shadows away from me.

Old men beneath the street
squat in catacomb cellars,
drinking chai, selling rugs:

Turkish, Iranian, Persian patterns
woven maps, unforgotten
transgressions, borders

made soft, blooming crimson
in silk loops pressed by a hundred
thousand steps.

Irbil is like Rome in this way,
like Athens, each city suturing
new skin to the skeleton.

And what passes
for ablution here:
splattering dust from rubble.

The woman coughs her black shoe
in the gravel again, disturbs
the dust with cherry seeds

and the hem of her dress.
Then laughing, she offers a cherry,
and slow Kurdish,
This was an Arab's house.

THE WAR MAKES EVERYONE LONELY

My sister had been receiving a lot of calls
from strangers. This is how she learns
her number is listed on an escort site.
Normally this is not the case.
Normally she talks about her fiancé,
her dog, what she thinks I must not want—
really—to hear.
                                But now these guys keep calling,
asking for Elisha. And I'm sitting there, in Afghanistan,
in a little plywood room painted red,
hung with pictures of the other guys' wives.
I can hear wind ribboning the concertina,
and Allen's boots on the roof as he brushes
snow off the dish, and two privates complaining
about guard shifts, debating the odds of an attack
tonight because nothing ever happens.
It's already 2 a.m., and cold as shit,
and nothing ever happens. And my sister
is thinking maybe she needs a lawyer,
and I'm thinking—what about Elisha?
Home, right now, counting hits
against the number of times the phone hasn't rung.

SEWING

Such eyes the widows in Corioli wear

Behind headlights drawing darker
night against the snow, I regret saying

kind of like Afghanistan aloud
with my mother and grandmother

in the otherwise silent heat of the car.
But back then too it had been spring.

All night I could hear the water running out.
Dirty snow returning to mud. Humvees crawling

thick tread into cliff roads. Prescott, swiveling
the roof-mounted Ma Deuce, saying

feels like my brother cheated on his wife
and now I have to give her flowers—

because the raids had been another team
and we were the ones arriving

in the villages of unglassed windows,
all of them asking *to whom are you beloved?*

Dressed like the men who killed
their husbands, we passed out sewing machines

to widows so they could make clothes
for their children and embroider cemetery flags.

My mother, my grandmother, the otherwise
silent heat. They wouldn't ask, but I answered.

It's just, we had to do a lot of slow driving.
At night. In the snow.

GOAT IN THE CLEARED VILLAGE

I did what I had always:
mangle grass and mud beneath my hooves,
between my dull-cornered teeth. Between
walled houses, orange blossoms
chimed in a green bower.
Barn thrush and sovereign kestrel
traversed second-story windows—
some open, some broken—on invisible thread.
I have nuzzled the wingspans of their dead,
their evaporating bones. I understood
their lightness as they feathered
the roasting smell of torched hashish
through the tree branches and green leaves
and the orange blossoms.
                                        In a poppy field,
a woman dipped her head, hiding.
There were ribbons fluttering
from palm trunks and dry poppies rattling.
There was gunfire. It doorwayed the morning.
There was gunfire, and it painted the wind red.
Whatever night left lingering lingered
in pieces—a clay bowl flowering the kitchen floor,
the sound of blood dragging fur, of holes
being made and refilled. I was the sound
of children running. Blue and cloud,
every alley ended in the sky, or iron gates

with red spray-paint Xs from the last time
these homes were made safe.
Cans of purple smoke swelled velvet sheets.
A soldier turned a doorway
into his silhouette, his barrel
exactly the size of my eye,
and leveled a fresh white X as he passed.

NOTICE AND FOCUS EXERCISE

In the army recruiting ad,
students will notice a young girl

hugging a soldier who might
be her dad or big brother.

They may note twenty-five
stars, four closed eyes,

three hands, one smile, one
black beret, one silver unit flash,

five instances of the word *army*,
six mentions of the word *strong*,

three fonts in four sizes.
They will note there are no guns

and no flags. Because they are
not asked to notice,

they will see no piles of feet
on airport roads

and no one assigned to shovel them.
No masked men on the roof

of a burning library eating
melons and yogurt, no men

carrying shovels that could
be RPGs, if shovels aren't enough.

No wild dogs fighting
in any fields of dead goats,

no banners or barbwire burial plots,
and no one watching the ridgeline.

No blistered trigger fingers.
No depressions in quiet skulls.

They will not notice the lack
of protesters in the street

firing Kalashnikovs, or praying
or mourning or running away,

nor the absence of rupture
scars in the road.

No dank hospital hallways.
No phantom limbs redacted.

No medals, or praying,
or running away.

THE COFFEE AISLE

You step back always
to boiling black froth in a tin cup,
to the density of flak-proof curtains
heavier than the air stirred up
by whatever is outside exploding,
whenever you arrive
among these *Colombian Supremos.*
These *Jamaican Blue Mountains,*
robust with floral notes and balanced
blends of pleasant acidity.
After disheveling homes
sunlit with tracks of finger-size holes
or rinsing blood from truck beds
after kneeling there long enough
your legs fell asleep, your fingers
in torn rubber gloves
in someone's torn leg,
anything that didn't taste like
dust was saffron or jasmine
held under the tongue.
But which of these mild
to moderate sharpnesses
can counterfeit best that flavor
when tamped into a cannon-mouth
French press here at home
in your undemolished kitchen?

AFTER STERILIZING THE CANTEENS

I'm sorry you asked if I liked
the taste you leave.
I'm sorry I answered
after hiking
so long in the quarry
we had to sterilize water.
I shouldn't have said
you were one
bursting seed
after another until the sink is full
of ripped-up
pomegranate skins
when I knew you
would have rather been marble
uncut in the sun,
a heavy table wine
and bay leaves, or
orange rinds scattered
over stones in a dry
creek bed. I'm sorry
this once
(the only time you've asked)
I was flailing for any lovely
thing that wasn't
silted water and iodine.

MY PITTSBURGH

For as long as I was gone, my Pittsburgh
was a summer city of telephone poles
tacked all over with beer-bottle caps.
Deer wandered Forbes Avenue
on their way to or from the river,
and no one was surprised
when lovers spent afternoons leaning
naked from bedroom windows calling
Marco— *Polo—*
while on their sills amber
glasses of iced tea emptied
and filled with sunlight.

When I came home there was snow.
Beautiful in the way beautiful
means absent, hoofprints appeared
often at crosswalks, but deer
were no longer seen.
Lovers spent the winter whispering
—Marco —Polo
back and forth in the cold parks
hoping to become vessels
for which *to pour into*
need not also mean pouring out,
until, lips pressed to their ears,
they heard each other saying only
—Marco —Marco —Marco

TELLING YOU I WILL DEPLOY AGAIN

I'll probably just open my mouth,
wait for something to fly out
the way, with a bat in the house, I spread
the front doors, turn on a few lights,
leave dark a path of open rooms,
and hope it follows.
                                        But sometimes they won't
so I snap them down with a tennis racket.
Scoop the shrieking things in a dustpan
and slough them outside. Regretting,
only a little, the need, the abrupt
cessation of a fragile thing,
that terrible satisfaction, even
with these apologies hanging limp,
crumpled in the rhododendrons.

DAYS OF 2009

This is the one where he leaves her, wrecks his sister's car after ten hours to Pittsburgh to see a girl who says he seems empty. And this is the one where he knots his shoulders over Arabic flash cards like a trash-can fire in his frozen barracks. The one where he watches the inauguration online whispering Arabic to himself. This is the one where he grows thankful to God on a long stretch of Virginia pike. Where he finds heaven is a highway—77 south-bound slack between mountains where nothing quits and the hills are frozen black waves full of terrible promise. The one where he's thankful for heaven and hateful it can only exist between things. Where Charleston and DC and Pittsburgh rise and recede like sewing needles. The one where he passes out in the pews of St. Matthew and thinks he's never seen anything so bright. So bright but not blinding. It's the one where he is wrong. The one where he learns to guess what he'll long for before he gives it up. This is the one where he gives it up.

POST 9/11 GAS TRAINING (1)

We practice putting on the masks,
being fast, and being bodies.
We had nine seconds from *gas! gas! gas!*,
then fifty meters down, and fifty meters back.
Slow draws carrying those of us fast
until the afternoon is gone and more
than half of us are dead. Though
none blood-shod, none drowning in air
—all better trained in panic.

HOW TO STAY AWAKE ON A TRAINING EXERCISE

Surroundeded by Carolina silence
and skeleton pines,
suck memory like a flask
filled with burning sips of her hand
closing the door.
With November midnight-deep
in its foxhole, frost
and quarter moonlight
gripping the gun barrels,
some guys take straight dips of instant
coffee between their gum
and lower lip, straining
bitterness through their teeth.
Rougher men
snort the grounds,
and those with nothing
sharp enough to remember
might lie with a knife
balanced under their chin.
Point gentle beneath them,
eyes buried in the dark.

SURVIVAL AND EVASION

Go ugly early

Day one: canteen cups of pine-needle tea.
Maggots on a roadkill buck. We thought
we knew how it would be. Had seen the skinny
trainees returning. Day three: Snickers
from the cab of a logging machine.
Heard dogs. Saw flashlights on the road.
Day nine: turned our tongues to chalk
with unripe persimmons. Used them to bait
a snare instead. Dug a pit for a fire. Dug a pit
for ourselves. Hid beneath branches to sleep.
Day eleven: the way it shrieked—figured
we'd caught a bird. Found a raccoon
dangling by its leg. Hissing spit. Reaching
still, for those rank persimmons,
while we looked for a thick enough branch.

SOMNAMBULANT

The barracks was Army-green wool
and white sheets turned down

to standard, six inches below the pillow,
a perfect perforated line

across every gray bunk frame
to the gray lockers lining the walls

and blocking the windows.
At night, the moon passed

through seams between the lockers,
flashing like a film reel

if you walked the dark room
fast enough. Now and then

on fire watch, when you were walking,
and the moon was flashing,

and the sheets were disheveled
by the sleepers, someone might jump

to attention, for some dreamt of
drill sergeant screaming.

I told her all of this when she found me
standing in the bedroom doorway.

Just order me back to bed.
We'll laugh about it in the morning
—she laughed then too.

BREACH

On my way to the airfield, then Texas,
then Bagram, I dropped my phone
beneath the driver's seat. The stoplight
swung like a tongueless bell. My fingers,
just comprehending a corner edge
of phone wedged between the seat
and center console, became my arm,
in up to the shoulder. Her warmth
claustrophobic as the Oklahoma sky
flattening those fields. A sunstruck, dry-rot
barn in the spreading high-plains wheat
and wandering herds of Anatolian Red,
where a veterinarian, myself, the pregnant
heifer were clay baking in a summer kiln.
Birthing chains drug from the truck bed
chattered like wind chimes being taken down
as I felt at two hooves pressed together—
praying, unprepared, and stupidly eager.

HOW TO STOP THE BLEEDING

A tourniquet will work
    unless it doesn't.

They don't always
    tell you what to do then

if the artery is torn
    behind the soft pocket

of an armpit, or thigh
    where it meets the pelvis,

where the external
    iliac becomes the femoral.

In that case, with gauze,
    pack the spaces

that could hold gallons
    if we had gallons.

Press a small wadding
    against the vessel.

One-for-one
    replace your fingers

with gauze, your fingers
    with gauze—To simulate:

take up a fistful of sand.
Walk into the ocean.

FIRST LIFE

Before the machine   is breathing for her
and I am replacing her head   on the gurney pillow,
occipital soft as a neonate's,   as an eggplant
rotting, I am praying   down the deep train tunnel of her
throat to see the pearlescent   triangle of vocal chords.

Before my civilian   chaperone can say
there it is,   saved your first life,
I am unpinching   my thumb and index
between her teeth,   conscious of their give,
like a practice dummy's   rigged to break when levered
too firmly   against a laryngoscope blade.

Before I am questioning   if ninety with brain cancer
and comatose now   still counts as saved
beneath portraits   of saints whose impassive
eyes shimmer like gilded fish   turning back and away in unison
and without explanation,   the chaperone is kneeling
next to the woman's coffee table   scabbed oxblood with candle wax,
offering me an endotracheal tube   prepped and lubed,
with reverence   I am placing it on her tongue.

MEDICS DON'T EARN KILLSTREAKS

Studying for exams, we played *Call of Duty*.
The fart stink of that barracks. Carpets of spilled beer.
Tourniquets and alcohol wipes in garbage bags
to be packed for the next day's IFAKs.
Rifles were weightless. Bombs fell with nothing
close to oversight. Injuries meant
heavy breathing
                    —a red-tinged screen.
A mini map showed us where the enemy were.
Four kills for a care package, five
for a care-package trap. Seven for a helicopter.
Eighteen to man its mini gun. I asked a Ranger
how many he'd needed to unlock a drone strike.
He said he mainly
                    stuck to the medicine.
Pressing *revive* before a progress bar runs out,
there's no difference between urgent and expectant.
No need to estimate under fire
the percentage of a body burned.
How much fluid to administer. How much per hour
they should piss out. No need to pull the bodies to cover.
They disappear without you
                              checking their pulse.

PASHTU REFRESHER

Zeh dodai khoram

We chant along in the armory classroom,
water bottles like votive candles
half full of toilet paper and dip spit,

teko dodai khorai

intoning each conjugation with the same
careful automation used to clean
our rifle parts,

hagoi dodai khoree

bolt scattered to its seven pieces
on a school desk, gun oil lubricating
an altar to the god of preparation.

Zeh dodai khoram
teko dodai khorai
hagoi dodai khoree

I eat food. You eat food.
We eat food like a charm
against ill will in all of its extremes.

CERTIFICATES OF TRAINING

I fucked up the certificates.
After a few misspellings
and formatting errors
only half of them ended up
on the good card stock,
scrawled with vineyard rows
of Pashtu rank, name,
and fathers' names.
No one cared.
After the ceremony,
photographs, blessings,
handshakes, and hands
held over the heart,
their Major only asked
if I would please
make new diplomas
in English. The Pashtu,
he said, is lovely
but unofficial.

INFORMANT

Why am I still waiting for you in that endless city?
Overhead doors pulled down on all the shops.
Darkness crowded with dog bark and sudden
clouds of thick, flammable-smelling sewer.
Afghan guards milled in the spotlight
generator's white noise, pretending to avert
their eyes from anyone they think I think is you.
Money for you in my pocket, I am trying
not to think about our last meeting. Your
cell-phone video. Hacksaw tugging neck skin.
The careful way you spoke in English
my uncle, my brother, my uncle's son. Your finger
touching each shemagh-wrapped face.
The one you couldn't name I knew was you.

DESERVING (I)

Preoccupied by the floorboards,
at a poetry reading
I saw a yellow jacket,
or maybe just a bee, struggling
with what I would call, in myself,
drunkenness—
wandering a bit, but never far,
indecisive and writhing
until lifted into the air.
Dragged, by a spider
hovering over it.
Not drunkenness then. Poison
or just plain tangling. I don't know
how a spider kills a bee.
I had heard engineers couldn't
improve a hornet's form
for efficiency, and I imagined
that perfect design
fighting a tether equally
strong and light.
It struggled a bit.
The poet continued:
Those with the time
for poetry don't deserve it.
The poetry or the time—
I wondered in that

small moment of my life,
in that whole life of the bee.

POST 9/11 GAS TRAINING (II)

To cultivate a sturdy faith in tear gas
we were introduced. *See that?*
Drill Sergeant Later grinned
at PRO PATRIA MORI stenciled red
above the cement-hut door,
Abandon hope when you enter here.
We knew not to enjoy his mistakes,
but I managed a moment, proud
for catching it. Then the entrance door
closing. A sergeant in MOPP gear stoking
tablets on a burner. CS tearing where
it found me. And all my pride became one
ragged panic.
                Somehow outside, somehow after
on my knees with everyone else, purging
years of sediment phlegm from scraped alveoli,
I saw the line waiting to go in, heard
the men behind me learning to drown.
Learning to breathe that evil pure as air.
Motes of gas, like dust in sunlight,
wafted from the exit labeled DULCE ET.

RANGE DETAIL

A lieutenant's mittened hand flapped
us into formation when the old range-control
civilian, probably a vet himself, arrived
to dip his boot toes in our mud.
What did we know then about mercy—
spilling mud from spent casings, stabbing
fingers stained carbon black, blunt-stubborn
after more shells in the trampling snow?
Set to picking brass on the machine-gun line
like sullen, wet chickens, we pecked metal
seeds into metal cans tapping nonsense ciphers.
Bitterness sounds like this: steel-tongued
cascades pouring out by the handful.
If he would admit we'd found enough brass,
there'd be a drowsy bus ride back to the barracks,
then civilian clothes and weekend leave
to tell exciting women in exciting bars that we
are soldiers, that we were shooting machine guns,
machine guns at nothing, and never
had we been sullen, wet chickens.
He stooped to sink the stiff beak of his fingers
into the mud, coming up with a clean, new bullet.
A 9 mm, a pistol round, glinting like a tooth on that
white field, in that gray air. We were murderous.
And he knew it, saying, *You boys always miss the last one.*

INDIANA-STAN

H. E. rounds look like kicked-up smoke-dust
the color of whatever earth they touch. Too far
to see but we know their noise and imagine
clouds when they bellow-thump bare hills
beyond the long since bombed-out
rust-hulks we were supposed to hit.
Then illume shells—packed light and smoke
and shot too low—drop phosphorous
through civilian fields we aren't
supposed to burn, so we wait down
the cease-fire in the bus that brought us.
Draw stick men fucking on fogged windows.
Press the meat of our fists to the glass.
Make baby feet. Over there, if the wheat
or poppy crops catch, we can leave
those fires as soon as they start.

TINDER PIC

I hope they see I'm laughing
even in the bomb pit
and don't just wonder
if I'm short and hiding
it with a low angle,
legs—let's not say redacted—
behind an impressive
pile of frag grenades
strung and vine ripened
like too-drab grapes
on coiled *det* cord,
their unpulled pins
still crimped to chrome
cylindrical blasting caps.
Behind claymore mines
in disciplined rows facing
front toward enemy inward,
I pose like the little teapot
with a mortar-round spout
tipping from my hand
at a jaunty angle.
Hope it all says: confident
and responsible.
As an aggressor
aware of his complicity.
Appreciates absurdity
and not afraid to get serious.

But there will be left swipes
for that arrogance.
For trying to play imperialist
and dissenter without seeming too
patriotic or worse—
apathetic. Naïve or too reckless.
Unwary and soon to explode.

CULTIVATING MASS

Let the peaceful young men work
their *bis* and *tris*. Let's not
begrudge them
their beach muscle.
Let them never need to Clean and Press
a casualty up over a Humvee's up-armor.
Let them never know a body
weighs more
unconscious or consider that barbells
are built to be lifted, our bodies
to lie down.

Today I can deadlift four-oh-five.
When I can move four-ten it will
not stop a bullet or
the overpressure of a bomb
flooding some tightened space, never mind
the shrapnel and the heat careening
through that rapid bloat
ripping—

But if lifting is not a prayer
against that
why do my knees hurt?
If the consecration of chalk buckets
is not a blessing,
then the measured tearing

down of tissue, the shallow scarring of muscle
is not teaching this body reverence
                                        to whatever
is in it demanding—cohere.

But I say this is faith.
I am learning to tighten myself
                                    knowing
how little good it will do.
                              Let the peaceful
          young men believe anything
                                            awhile longer.

DOWNED PILOT

No shit, there you were. Two holes the size of
quarters. Infected blisters divoting
each Achilles. Every step in those boots
was bloody, but you had been tasked, in twelve-
man teams, to transport two duffel bags stuffed
with 400 lbs. of sand—and some glass
bottles to make sure you set them down kindly.
Seven or eight clicks, you followed the route
turning at glow sticks duct-taped to traffic
cones. Carrying those imaginary men.
Those shoveled guts. Those thin, translucent bones
fracturing under their body's own weight.
You shouldered aluminum poles with sacks
of fake casualty swinging between them
and hated it. Hated those mute pilots.
Hated lowering them gently when you
wanted to drop. Hated that you had to
save them. Of course, you were the one who slipped—
crossing a man-made stream, an obstacle.
You can't remember the cold unhinging
your ankles. Only trying to get out
from under the poles. To roll the body
from the water. The sodden weight it gained.
How the bottles crunched. Their corners prodding.

If this were a war movie it would have
prepared you for some combat parallel,
some recurrence where the training paid off.
Maybe your partner force, the ANA,
would struggle to carry one of their own,
so you would step in, show em how it's done,
carry the shot man and lay your body
over his, shield him from the rotorwash.
And if he died, it wouldn't be from lack
of care. Or your fault. It was love you were
learning to carry. Love so clear and thin
it couldn't be seen. Only stumbled into.
Broken after having stepped so deeply
in the pieces. But you made them carry him
through the night to the HLZ. Told them
to hurry in the dark and be careful
setting him down so you could check his pulse.
You never lifted him once, made him walk
himself to cover after being shot.
This man you are credited with saving.

ON THE EVENING BEFORE MY DEPARTURE

—the first time—I kissed a man.
Who was crying. Who just wanted
to say I don't want you to leave.
It didn't matter I was just going to Texas.
Not the war. Not for another five weeks.
My friend like a balancing scale.
My friend with hands full of gin
and olives, whose beard tasted briefly
like brine and vermouth, needed it. I think
when he said kiss me he was saying
I'm tired of everyone going to war.

PRE-DEPLOYMENT CHAPLAIN'S BRIEF

Ahead of you is an unclean thing.
Do not be concerned with what you accomplish.

And who can bring a clean thing out
of an unclean? Not one, says Job.

But I counted all my days in jail,
and for that the days were long, slow tunnels.

Next time there will be no calendar.
After all, didn't Job also say:

His days are determined, the number
of his months are with thee?

He did. An accounting has been made
on your behalf. The figures are drawn.

You have been appointed those bounds
that you cannot pass.

So stay busy. Stay alive. Accomplish
as a hireling your day and don't
take count of anything.

THE ROAD TO POL-E-KHOMRI

may also be the road to Nahrain
or further

to Jang 'Ali, Na'man
and north

to Baghlan, Kunduz, and Bu'in.
Be wary,

to the south, you will meet Golbahar,
where bombs

are often heavy and shallow
buried.

No one will offer you shelter
in Ghazni

or Gardez. You will not sleep
until

Qalat-e Gilzay is well
behind you.

Though the road continues, you
will cease

in Kandahar—perhaps,
at last, a city you know.

TOURISTS

At the end of OEF thirteen, we visited Qala-i-Jangi.
That prison-fortress near Mazar-i-Sharif.

There was only one guard. He was happy
to lead us through the afternoon hay grass

still sifting bomb rubble. We took pictures
with him next to the memorial for the only casualty

whose name is recorded. I thought there were others:
shots of the guard at the entrance to the bunker

where the rioting prisoners were drowned;
with the purple loosestrife gathered

trembling against the walls; the walls
crumbling like aqueducts; the basement cells

cool and dark and quiet. I only found a few
of us—soldiers in civilian clothes, at the Blue Mosque,

pistols tucked behind our backs; of the tribal rugs
we bought afterward in the bazaar.

AUGURY

. . . a human need,
to give to shapelessness
a form.

They show us recordings of coalition
        convoys being attacked.

That car driving
        a bit too slow

before it evaporates
        and turns the afternoon

into a cordon?
        Watch for that.

A black horse, a white horse,
        a windmill spinning backward,

tea leaves, and chicken guts.
        In the trenches they thought

these might predict the bombs:
        that a Belgian might

switch horses or reverse a windmill
to mark artillery locations

and crowded hospitals.
How else to reason with it?

Now, a man might place a stone near the road
to mark a bomb

or signal for his relatives the turn
to reach his home.

Any exposed wire,
plastic jug,

even the mufflers strung up
like drying octopus

in front of the mechanics' shops
recognize some pattern,

as if anything could stop a bomb
recognizing its potential.

0300

Snow piling the perimeter wall.
Snow folded like clean towels on the low,
buried roofs of the mess, laundry, and the barracks.
A soft light frames the op-center door
like a winter postcard. In the cold, on the tower
I am only fingertips and earlobes, those
bits of flesh still exposed. I imagine myself
a glowing green eye in a gargoyle mass.
No longer concerned about attacks—
there will be no roads until the snow melts—
I stay awake, but I am not concerned.
The gusting cemetery flags are familiar now
and invisible at night. They carry no heat,
and I have given up mistaking them for men.
A wild dog saunters through the concertina
and burnt trash fishhooked in the razor wire.
A warm spot near the burn pit—maybe
in one of the ditches we dug to channel
claymore mines—he is a shadow glowing
darkly in the gray static of a thermal lens.
To my bare eye there is nothing
beyond these walls but night.

BLOCKING AN IMAGINED WAR MOVIE

Our camera should hang close behind the boy
with Baghlan province over his shoulder
scrolling the minivan window.
We should hear the Pashtu of his father and uncle,
the snoring of his grandfather. Then cut
to a perspective from a tower, down
a machine-gun barrel swaying from the father
to the uncle and grandfather all standing
outside the vehicle. Through the van window
two American soldiers approaching.
In subtitles: *Please.*
We have come here for your doctor. My son
has injured his knee. We have travelled six hours.

The doctor, who is not a doctor,
who is only a medic, is sent for.
A low angle, a view looking upward,
men and soldiers frame the shot. Moments pass.
Wind whistles. Dishdashas and rifle slings flap in the sound.
When the medic arrives, he speaks with the father,
crouches beside the boy seated in the sliding door.
He knows at a glance the knee is hopeless,
has been for years, but is unaware how cruel
to say so without at least pretending it might be
otherwise. We can see it doesn't take him long.
Now the van is driving away, and the boy going home

is not the boy who arrived. This boy knows more
surely his knee, gnarled and bunched like a root,
is not temporary. He will limp the rest of his life
to the well, to the shura, at harvest
shoveling the wind with grains and chaff.

MEDICAL REFRESHER

PowerPoint slides of algorithms
for shocking dysrhythmia back to clockwork,
drug dosages, and drip rate calculations,
the recommended ratio of bleach
to water for cleaning bloodstains,
and every thirty minutes, a *motivator*—
some clip to keep us awake, maybe get a laugh.

Now say that in one of these,
a man stands atop a train in a crowded station.
You can't hear him speaking,
but when he reaches above his head,
touching a cable of indeterminate wattage,
he poses there like Cicero declaiming,
and in his palm two puffs of light.

Then the cadre lean into their shtick:
This guy survives, actually. Yeah,
a team of Doctors Without Borders
was there waiting to board the train—

Now, say you've all seen this
one before but even still, wondering
what could be done for this life
made so abruptly a body, one of you
combat trained, not really doctors—
one of you soldiers—still asks, *really?*

FAILURE DRILLS

Two rounds center mass, one to the head.
Tap Tap Tap
Steady as a metronome. Our Bravo, Jon,
says *Squeeze—don't pull.*
Bring that shot group down. You want the sternum
to stop the bullet,
to splinter through the chest. And I see a cloud
of lacerations
blooming. Remember dipping a dental needle
into some kid's
forearm at Tampa General, years ago,
tapping for shards
of the car window he punched his arm through.
I took so long
he got bored. Walked from the hospital, right arm
still filled with glass.

***

Our captain is unimpressed by the M240's
inability to make spectacle
of a loading pallet propped at fifty meters.
We all are.
Green tip NATO rounds, even 7.62, only shiver
the wood-slat rib cage.
At Jon's direction I unbox the Carl Gustaf.
Prep antipersonnel

rounds—rockets full of barbed fléchettes.
Heavy and dense, each
detonation is a moment underwater.
They engulf us,
flaying the pallet with steel air until it finally falls.
But it falls
without destruction, so Jon anoints the wood with JP8,
pronounces *un-fucking-killable*
like a benediction. Grunts it again and again
on the way home,
in the back seat pulling fléchettes from his boot soles,
flicking them out the window.

A FABLE

One evening the cat spied a family
of mice hiding in a milk pail.
These will make a fine supper, he thought,
thrusting his face into the pail.
Lifting it, he soon had a mouthful of mice,
but found to his dismay the narrowing
neck of the pail narrowed also around his own.
His bulging cheeks kept him stuck fast,
and he could not swallow the mice. Even one.
He contorted with frustration. The mice tumbled
into and out of his mouth, and a soldier
fired a pistol. The cat held very still,
unwilling to remove his head lest any
of the mice escape. Unaware he had wandered
so close to a patrolled road. The soldier fired again.
Other soldiers laughed. The cat only dragged
erratic patterns with the pail, and no one knows
what became of the mice.

SHURA

Have I told you we met a man in Iraq
calling himself king of the Kawliya?
He hosted a dinner. We sat on the floor.
Peeled meat from goat bones. Ate dolma
stuffed plump with eggplant and beef.
Pinched teacups of sugar, settled as fine
as river silt,
                    and skimmed chai from the surface.
The king said he liked the Kurds for giving
him if not citizenship at least land
on which to host, and if not jobs at least access
here to water. He said Iran is lovely
and no matter what anyone else may say
larger than Texas,
                              larger than half of America.
The king said we should smoke and we smoked.
He said eat and we learned eating
all of what is offered suggests wanting more.
He said it is respect to feed another
from your hand. I remember my fingernail
against a man's lip.
                              I don't know what he remembers.
Outside we sat in a council of lawn chairs.
The king said smoke and we smoked. The desert sky
rolled away into dark. Our bodyguards watched
from their vehicles. In unlit windows the faces of children

luminous and brief.
                                        Then a chair beneath the king collapsed.
Slowly as if melting. He laughed. And we laughed.
We laughed the sound of flags snapping.
We laughed the sound of sand shaken from a boot,
of steel shovels glancing stones.
                                                            It's good luck,
he told us, breaking a chair. And inside,
the women who had prepared our food
and waited with their children for us to finish
were given to eat what we had left.

DAYS OF SPRING, 2016

Another year refusing water to children.
When they made the universal gesture for thirst
along roadsides you wouldn't stop.
Could not, you said to no one.

A bombing at the gate before you arrived
was just a story you knew about rubble.
Passing through, you waved at the guards
hired to die so you wouldn't when another bomb came.

Afternoons, you worked with the physical therapist
learning to scrape sore tissue
with a slice of machined steel
curved to match the shape of the musculature.
Like a cradle or scythe, you said to no one.

At night, Armenian contractors in rooftop
sandbag nests did not murmur or snore in moonlight.
But you heard the smoke deserting
their thin cigarettes, and they annotated
their watch log when your Styrofoam to-go box
squeaked across the courtyard to the room
where you ate alone watching sun-dried
bricks of opium dissipate their phosphorescent
heat into distant courtyards and the same
moonlight of that still somehow sacred country.

And that was how morning found you,
sometimes a cradle, sometimes a scythe,
bright as the nights were silent.

CAPABILITIES BRIEF

Incandescent, indistinct, some brightness
in a carrot garden
buries its hands again and again.
Earth plumes
like sand under clear water.
The sizzle reel
of drone footage set to Taylor Swift
continues. The pilots
ask us to save questions for the end.

Two men hold hands walking a path at night,
luminescent together
in what must seem, to them, like the dark.
Two men
become one pillar of flame, one bush
burning
in a brief and sudden rapture.
No audio
but impact in static-gray
dirt jumping just off the beat. Impact
in the camera shuddering.

A figure squats to pray, dial a bomb nestled
in a drainage ditch.
Watched by something unseen but felt, it must be
faith

to go out, still, into the cloudless dark
and shit
beneath the almond trees and stars and the slow night
circling—

And when we cease circling. When the lights tick on
and we cease
to be the long slow night. We go out
into sunbright Texas,
tobacco juice hissing on the tarmac.
Someone says
I can't believe they made us listen to Taylor Swift.
And someone says
I can't believe it only carries two bombs.
And someone says
hot enough out here, if we had eggs—
and he spits again.

0500

Breath dissolves into morning fog, and a fox
emerges from the mist-heavy mouth of a wadi.

Is this difficult—is life harder for a fox here
than for a fox somewhere else?

My team sergeant likes the phrase
perception of inequality,

as in the privates wouldn't mind sharing a barracks
so much if we didn't have our own rooms—

We both hear the dogs
sound their desperate bells, and she,

the fox, flickers away like a signal fire
licking foothills toward the mountains.

Easier to follow the bulk of hounds
hurling dirt and dragging ribs.

I guess I'd like to see them catch her. The pleasure
they'd take in a bloody muzzle, but more I want to

know if she lives easier after. Remembering
how good things were before the hounds.

DESERVING (II)

After a photograph by Emilien Urbano

Did the killers, or at least
                                        the men assigned
to dump the bodies,
                              consider composition?
How best for symmetry
                                   and depth of field to heap
two corpses, carpet-wrapped,
                                        amid the brown field's
furrow, its straw grass?
                                   Did they think about the parallel
arch of tire tracks,
                              how they'd texture the earth
and flatten the sky?

                              No—not carpets,
blankets, fleece synthetics
                                        gleaming contours of sunlight
among their wine-maroon tangles,
                                             diluted gold, and lavender.

Blankets or carpets, regardless.
                                             Regardless, the light—bodies
sloughed in a field then photographed.

In their repose
deserving more than this poem
and its portions
of sky framed by power lines.
Its telephone poles
like tall crosses
receding.

HOW TO TRANSITION A PROVINCE

We named the region self-sustaining
and ended an eight-month occupation

frightening children from the burn pit,
petitioning elders not to send them

after imagined valuables in our refuse.

We fed our squat, dirt-bunkered camp
to a hired backhoe. Invited the village

to come and to take. Among our flattened clapboard
walls and yellow cinder-block foundations

their silence settled like a murmuration landing.

Our sandbags were cut and dropped like ballast.
Our umber and empty oil drums,

mattresses still plastic-wrapped,
my canted plywood writing desk,

all the small corners in that small base

were pulled open. Picked blessedly clean.
Before our dust-wake settled, no stone,

if we had stacked it, was left standing on another.

SELF-PORTRAIT WITH WEDDING, VINEYARD, AND GUNSHOT

I doubted anyone could really tell
the distance and direction of incoming
fire, all those nights of patrol and ambush,
learning to hustle hundred-pound rucks
through the woods on hand signal and whisper.
Somewhere in the dark, OPFOR broke open
their blank ammunition, and I just yelled
what everyone else was yelling. *Two o'clock!*
Three hundred meters! But when the bride said *oh*,
and the owner said *kids*, and everyone went
back to ringing their champagne flutes,
I remembered passing, not far back,
a deer downed at the roadside, a sheriff's car
slowing—could have pointed, right then, to his gun.

UNPRACTICED

Walking outside after, I stepped on a snake
and thought *copperhead*. The way I think
every insect droning is a cicada.
But it did look like a dusty string
of penny shavings even dead.
I remembered back in training, a soldier
squirming in the dirt. Shot pretend-dead
in a fictional ambush. When he fell, he fell wrong—
found a little copperhead with his hand.
I've heard the babies can't control themselves.
All the poison. All at once. Who can say
if that snake then went on to starve
for lack of venom. If one drop more
than it intended bled.
                                        But if I come to anger
like that. Without practice. Without saving
anything to live on. Don't forgive me.

EVERYTHING IN SUNLIGHT I CAN'T STOP SEEING

We leave my sister's house, and the intersection
transformer is still humming somehow. I'm used to
electricity quieting in the wire when the sun
scrapes its knee bloody up the mosque steps
and the cupolas and dusk emerge suddenly
from knots of cable hulking over alleyways
like hornets' nests,
                                        but here in DC
we walk beneath clean lines, orange and white
fluorescent streetlamps turning the air around
themselves resinous with bluing rings like flooded
drainage ditch ripples circling a dropped pair
of earrings. Flashbacks
                                             don't announce themselves.
It takes so little. I want to say the hinged arm
of a driver-side mirror balled with plastic wrap
looks like a reckless stump dressing: feral,
ready to ravel corybantic from an iron sight,
or litter hinge, or protruding bolt pinning
together a helicopter's cicada husk—
                                                              because it does,
but then you might imagine, or imagine me
imagining, a casualty's arm lifted, pointing,
smoke-cloud of hand exposed, drawn
dissipating into the rotor wash,
                                                        and that never happened

to me. Meanwhile, tree branches, black
in the dawn sky, resume their grays and browns
by lunch. The black wrought fences continue
leaning into their rust, rigid and failing, and there
is no war in this but me.

NOTES

“What’s It Like?”: The epigraph comes from Paul Fussell’s *The Great War and Modern Memory* (New York: Oxford University Press, 1975), 213.

“Aubade between Deployments”: MAT-V is shorthand for a mine-resistant all-terrain vehicle.

“Sewing”: The epigraph comes from Shakespeare’s *Coriolanus* (2.1). Ma Deuce is a colloquial name for the Browning M-2 .50-caliber machine gun.

“Survival and Evasion”: Trainees at the US Army Survive, Evade, Resist, and Escape (SERE) school are told “go ugly early” and encouraged to eat unpalatable food early in a survival situation rather than waiting until they are desperate.

“Medics Don’t Earn Killstreaks”: IFAK is an acronym for an individual first-aid kit.

“Informant”: A shemagh is a traditional Middle Eastern headdress fashioned from a square scarf.

“Deserving (I)”: The italicized line is taken from the poem “Breaking Spring” by Matt Hart.

“Post 9/11 Gas Training (II)”: MOPP is an acronym for mission-oriented protective posture used in toxic environments. CS is a common ingredient in tear gas.

"Indiana-stan": H. E. stands for high-explosive.

"Tinder Pic": Det cord or detonating cord is a high-speed fuse that explodes (rather than burns); it is used in detonating high-yield explosives.

"Downed Pilot": ANA stands for Afghan National Army. HLZ stands for helicopter landing zone.

"Tourists": OEF stands for Operation Enduring Freedom.

"Augury": The epigraph to this poem comprises three lines that close Carl Phillips's poem "Fray."

"Blocking an Imagined War Movie": A dishdasha is an ankle-length Arab garment, similar to a robe, usually with long sleeves.

"Failure Drills": "Bravo" refers to the US military occupational specialty code for a Special Forces Weapons Sergeant, in charge of weapons training. An "enfilade" is directed gunfire along the length of a target. "Carl Gustaf" refers to an 84 mm portable, reusable anti-tank recoilless rifle. And "JP8" is shorthand for jet fuel, used as a diesel fuel replacement in military vehicles.

"Deserving (II)": This poem was inspired by Emilien Urbano's photograph *The Bodies of Two Yazidis, Killed by the Islamic State, Sinjar, Iraq, August 2014*.

"Self-Portrait with Wedding, Vineyard, and Gunshot": OPFOR stands for opposing force, a military unit tasked with representing the enemy for training purposes.